DEVELOPING WORLD

D1102934

CHINA AND BEIJING

PHILIP STEELE

W
FRANKLIN WATTS
LONDON•SYDNEY

DEVELOPING WORLD

CHINA AND BEIJING

W
FRANKLIN WATTS
LONDON•SYDNEY

Franklin Watts

Published in 2016 by the Watts Publishing Group
An imprint of Hachette Children's Group
Part of the Watts Publishing Group
Carmelite House
50 Victoria Embankment

An Hachette UK company
www. hachette.co.uk
www.franklinwatts.co.uk

ISBN 978 1 4451 4955 4
Dewey number: 951.06

Series Editor: Julia Bird
Series Advisor: Emma Epsley, geography teacher and consultant
Series Design: sprout.uk.com

Picture credits:

Mira Agrou/Dreamstime: 39br. Andersen/Dreamstime: 15tl. Andrey Bayda/Shutterstock: 40. Natalie Behring/Aurora Photos/
Alamy: 16. Bjshanshan/Dreamstime: front cover t. Chameleonseye/Shutterstock: 20b. Hung Chung Chih/Shutterstock:
14t, 18. Chungking/Shutterstock: 6. Pierro Crucuatti/Shutterstock: 19, 33. EPA/Alamy: 12, 13. Eprom/Dreamstime: 11.
5dmarkii/Dreamstime: 38b. Gary718/Shutterstock: 9. Svilen Georgiev/Shutterstock: 21t. Hannamariah/Shutterstock: 31t.
Robert Harding PL: 39t. Imagine China: 17, 27. Interfoto/Alamy: 8. Jianbinglee/Dreamstime: 31b. Keystone USA-ZUMA/
Rex Features: 42. Lidacheng/Dreamstime: 25t. Liumantiger/Dreamstime: 26. Mamahoohooba/Shutterstock: 23. Meanma-
chine77/istockphoto: 15bl. Paop/Dreamstime: 22. Xiao Peichen/Dreamstime: 43. Jack Q/Shutterstock: 34. Cora Reed/Shut-
terstock: 37. Reuters/Corbis: 41. Sergei/Dreamstime: 35b. Lee Snider/Dreamstime: 39bl. Spirit of America/Shutterstock: 20t.
Keren Su/Corbis: 25b. Alvin Teo/Dreamstime: 36. Testing/Shutterstock: 10. TonyV3112/Shutterstock: 15tr, 21b, 30, 32, 38t.
Xinhua/Rex Shutterstock: 28. Yun Yang/Dreamstime: 24. Guo Yu/Shutterstock: 14b. Liu Yu/Corbis: 35t. Xi Zhang/Dream-
stime: front cover b. Liang Zhao/Dreamstime: 15br

Every effort has been made by the Publishers to ensure that the websites on page 45 of this
book are suitable for children, and that they contain no inappropriate or offensive material.
However, because of the nature of the Internet, it is impossible to guarantee that the contents
of these sites will not be altered. We strongly advise that Internet access is supervised by a
responsible adult.

Printed in Malaysia

CHINA AND BEIJING

CONTENTS

INTRODUCING CHINA

CHINA AND CHANGE

Skyscrapers of glass and steel rise from the city skylines. Tall cranes tower above construction sites. The railway stations are crowded with workers, the traffic roars by hotels and banks and airports. Tourists fly in to take photos of the Great Wall of China or Beijing's old Imperial Palace.

Today's visitors to China take such sights for granted, but 50 years ago, city traffic was mostly made up of bicycles, and most of the population lived in country villages. Few foreigners travelled here. From the 1990s onwards, this large Asian nation rapidly moved from poverty to riches. Today its amazing spurt of growth has slowed down, and China's economic future has become less certain.

CHINA GOES GLOBAL

Even so, China still has the world's second largest economy after the United States of America and is a major military power. China is also heavily involved in business and manufacturing around the world, from Europe to Africa and South America. Whatever direction the Chinese economy takes in the future, it is certain to affect the lives of people in many other countries.

The Oriental Pearl TV Tower soars 468 metres above Shanghai's Pudong district. Before the 1990s this was an undeveloped area of docks and fields.

RUSSIA

KAZAKHSTAN

MONGOLIA

ALTAI MTS

TIAN SHAN MTS

Urumqi

KYRGYZSTAN

XINJIANG UYGHUR

AJIKISTAN

TAKLAMAKAN DESERT

CHINA

Harbin

Beijing

Tianjin

NORTH KOREA

SOUTH KOREA

Yellow Sea

JAPAN

Huang He (Yellow River)

Da Yunhe (Grand Canal)

Xian

East China Sea

GHANISTAN

AKISTAN

TIBET

Chengdu

Suzhou

Shanghai

HONG KONG

Lhasa

Chongqing

Wuhan

Hangzhou

HIMALAYA MOUNTAINS

Chang Jiang (Yangtse)

NEPAL

EVEREST

BHUTAN

Fuzhou

INDIA

BANGLADESH

Guangzhou

Xiamen

TAIWAN

Zhu Jiang (Pearl River)

BURMA
(MYANMAR)

VIETNAM

Shenzhen

LAOS

HAINAN

South China Sea

PHILIPPINES

THAILAND

SRI LANKA

MACAU

A TRIP TO CHINA

The People's Republic of China is big and beautiful. It takes up nearly 9.6 million square kilometres of eastern Asia, with bitterly cold winters in the north, but a warm and humid sub-tropical climate in the south. Floods, earthquakes and typhoons are common.

Western China is bordered by some of the world's highest mountain ranges, including the Himalayas. There are remote, harsh deserts such as the Taklamakan and the wide open grassy steppes of Inner Mongolia.

In the eastern half of China, two long, broad rivers, the Huang He (Yellow River) and the Chang Jiang (Yangtze), flow eastwards across great plains to the sea. The soil here has been farmed and built upon for thousands of years and most Chinese people still live on these plains and coasts. China has the highest population on the planet, home to over 1.367 billion people. One in five humans living today are citizens of China.

VITAL STATS

CHINA FULL NAME: People's Republic of China
• AREA: 9,596,961 sq km • POPULATION: 1.367 billion • CAPITAL: Beijing (22 million)
• BIGGEST CITY: Shanghai (24 million)
• SPECIAL ADMINISTRATIVE REGIONS: Hong Kong, Macau • LONGEST RIVER: Chang Jiang/ Yangtze (6,418 km) • HIGHEST MOUNTAIN: Qomolangma/Everest (8,848 m) • NATURAL RESOURCES: Coal, iron ore, oil, natural gas, tin, tungsten, uranium

PEOPLE AND NATION

Qin Shi Huangdi was the first emperor of a united China. He died in 210 BCE.

PAST TO PRESENT

The rapid changes taking place in China today are not happening in some new country. They are rooted in one of the oldest civilisations on Earth. China has a long history of innovation. Chinese inventors first gave the world paper, gunpowder, printing and compasses.

AN ANCIENT EMPIRE

China became a single empire in 221 BCE and remained under the strict rule of emperors until the 1900s. China was often inward-looking and locked in tradition, but at other times it engaged with the rest of the world. For many centuries goods such as tea and silk were traded overland to western Asia and Europe.

By the 1700s and 1800s, China was being overtaken by the new industrial nations of Europe. Weak emperors gave away control of key Chinese cities and ports to foreigners. In 1912 the last emperor, Puyi, was overthrown and China became a republic.

YEARS OF TURMOIL

Troubled years lay ahead. Warlords, leaders with private armies, seized control in some regions. Communists, seeking to give power to poor peasants and workers, battled with the Nationalists. In the 1930s, neighbouring Japan invaded many areas. By 1949 the Communists controlled all of China and the Nationalists had fled to the island of Taiwan, forming a rival government. The new Communist state faced hostility from the USA and its allies.

THE PEOPLE'S REPUBLIC

The People's Republic of China faced many problems in its early years, grounded in centuries of poverty and social injustice. Communist leader Mao Zedong (1893-1976) nationalised industry so that it was run by the state. He took farmland from landlords and gave it to the peasants, who had to take part in shared farming projects. The changes, known as the Great Leap Forward, were radical, and often resulted in violence and great hardship. Some Communist Party members called for a change of direction. They were accused of betrayal by more radical members, who idolised Mao. In the 1960s this led to a period of chaos and strife.

NEW ORDER

When Mao died in 1976, a new leader named Deng Xiaoping changed China's economic policy and brought in foreign investment. Relations with the West improved. This new China was turning out to be very different from the one Mao had envisaged. It was the start of the China we know today.

A portrait of Mao Zedong still overlooks the gateway to Beijing's Imperial Palace.

9

MEET THE PEOPLE

In the big Chinese cities, people love to crowd around a table, to chat and argue and joke. People in China's cities have always lived at close quarters with their neighbours, sharing space. The Special Administrative Region of Macau is the most densely packed territory in the world, with 19,053 people to each square kilometre, making it over four times as crowded as London.

POPULATION PRESSURE

China's population is expected to peak at about 1.5 billion in 2033. All those people need food and use up precious resources, such as water. Careful planning is necessary. Censuses have been held in China for over 2,000 years, but surveying today's vast population is a difficult task. In 2010 it took 6.5 million temporary officials to check about 400 million households! The census confirmed that the rate at which the population was growing had slowed down.

PLANNED FAMILIES

In 1979 China tried to solve its soaring population problem by restricting most city-dwelling parents to having a single child. This caused unhappiness and social problems. The population aged as the workforce numbers became limited. In November 2015 the law was changed so that all parents could have two children.

People go shopping in crowded downtown Macau,
a Special Administrative region of China.

BOYS OR GIRLS?

A preference for boys is traditional in a land which relies on manual labour for income. Since the scanning of pregnancies became common, there has been an increase in the illegal abortion of girl babies. There may be about 119 boys being born for every 100 girls in some regions. This is a humanitarian tragedy, and could lead to a generation of Chinese men being unable to find wives in the future.

PEOPLES AND LANGUAGES

Over nine out of 10 Chinese belong to the Han ethnic group. The rest belong to 55 smaller groups, with different customs, beliefs and languages. These minorities are called nationalities. They make up a small proportion of the total, but they occupy over half of the land area. Tensions between ethnic groups are often high, especially in the far northwest and in Tibet, where many people oppose Chinese rule and settlement by Han Chinese.

The main language of the state is called Putonghua or Standard Chinese, also known as Mandarin. Many other variants and dialects of Chinese are spoken across China however, as well as some very different languages, such as Mongolian, Tibetan and Uyghur.

A new baby faces a new China. What will the future hold?

WHO GOVERNS?

Before he became Chinese leader, Xi Jinping had already visited the United States to discuss trade with President Barack Obama.

LEADING MAN

In 2012 a new Chinese leader stepped onto the red-carpeted stage at the Great Hall of the People in Beijing. He was called Xi Jinping (pronounced SHEE jin BING) and had been chosen as General Secretary of the Communist Party of China (CPC). Xi had won control of the world's biggest political party, with over 80 million members. Big screens on the street showed Xi's speech, but most Chinese people knew little about him. They probably knew his wife, a popular singer called Peng Liyuan, rather better. Confirmed as President in 2013, Xi described his political vision as the 'Chinese Dream'. He brought many powers under his supervision and introduced economic, legal and military reforms. He has played an important part in international politics, but has seen growing strains in relations between Japan and China.

HOW POLITICS WORKS

The Communist Party of China controls China's political system. Although there are eight other small parties, they are all in alliance with the CPC. There are no free elections between competing parties. Within the CPC, members often hold very different opinions and behind the scenes different factions jostle for power.

In China citizens over 18 can vote every five years for Local People's Congresses. The members who are elected vote for a National People's Congress (NPC) which chooses the officials who make the laws. Women have played a much more prominent part in Chinese society since 1948, but few reach the top jobs. The key roles in the CPC are still mostly held by men.

CORRUPTION IN CHINA

As soon as Xi Jinping took power, he promised to tackle corruption. Dishonesty has been a serious problem in the Communist Party and government for many years. Bribery, illegal property rackets and fraud are common. Government contracts are often awarded to friends or relations. People with powerful connections may escape prosecution for a crime. Rising public anger makes Xi's anti-corruption campaign a priority.

Corruption reaches right to the top. Su Shulin, a former oil and gas executive and the governor of Fujian province, was investigated in October 2015 over allegedly corrupt dealings.

OUTSIDE THE NPC

China has regional governments in its provinces and city-based municipalities. Autonomous regions, having a separate ethnic identity, are given greater powers to make their own laws. Hong Kong and Macau are former colonies of Britain and Portugal. They are called Special Administrative Regions and have their own political and legal systems.

CHINA AND COMMUNISM

The Chinese party system is typically communist, but China's economic policies are not. Communism aims to ensure that working people receive the full reward for the things they make or the work they do. Profits should not be paid to investors and shareholders so that they can accumulate private wealth, or capital. Capitalism was bitterly opposed under Mao Zedong, but China now welcomes private companies making profit. However the state or regional governments still own many companies and direct the economy.

FOCUS ON BEIJING

ANCIENT CITY

Beijing may not be China's biggest city and it has not always been the national capital, but for much of its history it has been a great centre of political power. Decisions taken here still affect the whole of this vast country, just as they did when emperors ruled China from Beijing's Imperial Palace. This complex of splendid halls and spacious courtyards, behind red walls and a moat, forms a city within the city.

On a frosty winter's day the tiled roofs of Beijing's historical palaces and temples look glorious in the sun. Soaring against a blue sky you may see colourful kites, tugged by icy winds blowing all the way from Mongolia. Chinese visitors and overseas tourists throng the city's ancient monuments, or travel north of the city to visit ancient tombs or the Great Wall of China.

However concrete high-rise buildings and expressways have now replaced most of old Beijing, and filled in its tree-lined canals. The streets are filled with people hurrying to work and with chaotic traffic. More and more city dwellers drive cars, so exhaust fumes often create a hazy smog which hangs in the air. Welcome to Beijing, a city of constant change. Its municipality, the greater urban district, is home to over 22 million people.

The old Imperial Palace is known as the Forbidden City, because ordinary people were not allowed to pass inside its gates or even to glimpse the emperor.

Tiantan, the beautiful Temple of Heaven, dates back to the 1400s. The emperors used to come here to pray for a good harvest.

Tiananmen Square is a huge area bordering the Imperial Palace and the massive Great Hall of the People. In 1989 it was at the centre of political protests demanding democratic reform, but these were brutally put down.

Modern Beijing has become a city of high-rise housing, international hotels, offices and factories.

The traditional housing for the ordinary folk of Beijing was made up of low buildings around a courtyard, bordering narrow lanes and alleys. Most of these 'hutongs' are now gone.

The National Stadium built for the Beijing Olympics in 2008 was immediately nicknamed 'the Bird's Nest'! The successful Olympic Games presented a new image of the city to the world, but about 300,000 people lost their homes to make way for construction.

LAND AND WORK

MAKING A LIVING

About 33 per cent of China's workers farm the land, while 30 per cent have jobs in factories or mines. Most of the remainder find work providing services, such as nursing, teaching or office jobs. Working long hours in a hotel may be tiring, but for many it offers an easier life than in the farming village back home, and the work is better paid.

BOOM AND AFTER

China's economic growth over the last 25 years has been spectacular. China has the second biggest GDP, after the USA, and it is the world's top exporter, shipping out electronic equipment, machinery, clothing, furniture, plastics, medical goods, cars and steel. A fall in demand worldwide and a changing market inside China has slowed that growth. Even so, it is still the world's fastest growing economy.

Over 3,000 workers produce garments at a factory in Longnan, central China, owned by Hong Kong based Top Form International.

SHENZHEN SUPERLATIVES

Before 1979 Shenzhen, to the north of Hong Kong, was little more than a village. It was then developed by the government as a Special Economic Zone to attract foreign investment. That village has become a high-rise city, part of a booming industrial region around the Zhujiang or Pearl River delta.

- Today the zone is home to 15 million people.
- Shenzhen's industries include computer software, electronics, chemicals and telecommunications.
- Shenzhen's US$3 trillion stock exchange is connected with Hong Kong and Shanghai.

A worker at a coal mine in northwest China. China is the biggest coal producer in the world, but the work is poorly paid and can be dangerous.

THE POVERTY GAP

China's economic boom created many millionaires, and a wider class of managers whose wages may equal those paid in the USA. Although the number of Chinese people living in poverty has been greatly reduced in recent years, a gulf has opened up between the richest and poorest in society. The top fifth in society earn almost half of the national income, while the bottom fifth get under five per cent of it. For the unemployed, poor labourers or peasant farmers, prosperity remains a distant dream.

17

TOWN AND COUNTRY

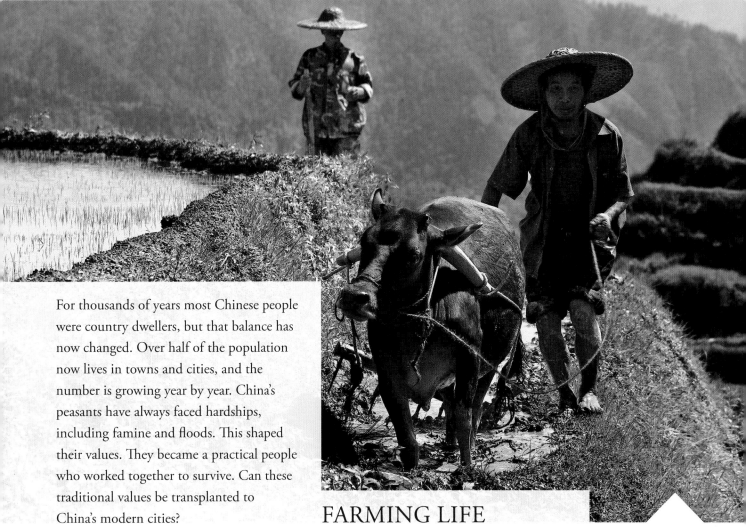

For thousands of years most Chinese people were country dwellers, but that balance has now changed. Over half of the population now lives in towns and cities, and the number is growing year by year. China's peasants have always faced hardships, including famine and floods. This shaped their values. They became a practical people who worked together to survive. Can these traditional values be transplanted to China's modern cities?

FIELDS AND VILLAGES

Many Chinese villages are made up of small cottages, perhaps built of clay brick or concrete with tiled roofs. Pigs, ducks and chickens wander in the street and corn cobs or chilli peppers are hung up to dry. Every scrap of land is cultivated, even in mountainous regions.

FARMING LIFE

In the north there are fields of millet and wheat, with orchards growing apples or Chinese pears. The misty hills of west central China are often bright yellow with oilseed rape. Lakes and rivers are fished with line and net. The farming year is an exhausting routine of ploughing, planting, hoeing, reaping and threshing. Southern landscapes include terraced hillsides for growing tea and paddy fields for wet rice cultivation, with wallowing water buffalo.

Farmers work on the Dragon's Backbone rice terrace in Longsheng County, Guangxi. They can earn about £500 per year.

URBAN SHIFT

Since 1985 the gap in income between country and town has risen by 68 per cent, so it is no wonder that many rural workers have moved to the cities to find work. By 2010 the census showed that 220 million Chinese had worked away from their home for over six months of the year.

LIFE IN THE CITY

Even at the height of the economic boom, migrant workers from the country often had a tough time in the big cities. Those who found work often received low pay, which had to be sent to their families back home. The recent slowdown of the economy has resulted in factory closures. Some migrant workers are now heading back to the countryside.

For wealthier city dwellers, there are high-rise, well furnished apartments, with the latest televisions and washing machines. Fashionable clothes and eating out at restaurants are all options. These would have been unheard-of luxuries not so long ago.

East Nanjing Road in Shanghai, part of one of the world's busiest commercial centres.

FOCUS ON BEIJING

FINANCIAL HUB

Beijing makes money. Modern hotels cater for the many tourists who come here to explore the city and visit the Great Wall. The capital is a centre for banking, insurance and finance. Here too are the headquarters of many big Chinese and international companies. The chief business districts are along Financial Street and in the Guomao area. New electronic and computer technology is developed in the Zhongguancun district. There are expensive shopping malls and car sale rooms.

But most of the people on the city streets are on modest or low incomes. They have all sorts of jobs – waiters, road sweepers, labourers, bus drivers, cooks or traders in the city's many markets. As elsewhere in China, there are great differences in income and working conditions, with many migrant workers from the countryside on low pay and experiencing poor working conditions.

Beijing's industries include iron and steel, chemicals, oil refinery, electronics, telecommunications and information technology. Factories are mostly sited on the outskirts of the city, but some of the dirtiest ones have been relocated in a bid to clean up the air. Vegetables are grown in the suburbs and crops such as wheat and maize are supplied from the surrounding countryside.

A baker sells buns in one of the few remaining hutong districts (see page 15) in Beijing. Street vendors are always busy in Beijing, from breakfast until night time. Steamed dumplings, egg pancakes and buns stuffed with pork are all popular snacks.

Most of Beijing's traditional hutongs have been demolished, but renovation offers work for bricklayers. A skilled builder can earn about £12.80 for a 10-hour day.

Cut flowers grown in the warm south go on sale at the end of January in Ditan Park, Beijing. A flower seller's busiest time is at Chinese New Year (the Spring Festival).

Beijing has about 67,000 taxis, contributing to the traffic congestion. Taxi drivers in Beijing often work a 14-hour day, over the legal limit. The company they work for can take a large share of their fares.

21

ON THE MOVE

A nation the size of China needs to keep its wheels turning. It cannot function without good communications. Over the last 60 years Chinese engineers have been pushing road and rail links through remote, difficult terrain. The 2006 rail link with Tibet reaches an altitude of 5,072 metres.

CHINA BY TRAIN

Most long journeys within China are taken by train, and railways also shift large amounts of freight. Stations are thronged with people, especially over Chinese New Year, when workers return home to their families, clutching bags full of gifts. Express trains offer several classes of travel, from the crowded 'hard seats' to the more comfortable 'soft sleepers'.

CAR MAD

China has over 3.8 million kilometres of roads, but the real transport revolution is taking place on city streets. Towns used to swarm with bicycles, as few people could afford to own cars. Now China is in love with the petrol engine and manufactures one out of every four cars produced in the world. Taxi cabs, motorcycles, minibuses, lorries and buses add to city traffic jams and pollute the air.

Harsh terrain. National Highway 219 is one of the world's highest motorable roads. It crosses from Xinjiang-Uyghur Autonomous Region into Western Tibet.

The high-speed Shanghai Maglev (magnetic levitation) train uses magnets to glide above the track.

RIVER PORTS

China has more navigable waterways than any other country. Da Yunhe, the Grand Canal, has carried north-south traffic for over 1,500 years. River steamers carry passengers from Chongqing down the Chang Jiang all the way to Shanghai. Downstream dams are bypassed via locks with extreme drops. Traditional wooden boats carrying local produce can be seen alongside barges, bulk carriers and car transporters.

INTERNATIONAL LINKS

Most overseas visitors arrive in China by plane. Beijing is the world's second busiest airport and offers internal flights all over China. Arrivals at Shanghai airport are whisked into the city by a futuristic Maglev train with a top speed of 431 kph. China's economy also depends on many big international seaports around eastern and southern coasts, designed to handle ferries, oil tankers and container ships.

BUILDING BRIDGES

When the Venetian merchant Marco Polo visited the Chinese city of Suzhou in 1276, he wrote that the city had 6,000 stone bridges! The Chinese are still building bridges today.

A complex of sea bridges across the Jiazhou bay, in Shandong province, opened in 2011. It links the city of Qingdao with neighbouring districts and islands and is earthquake-proof. The total length of the bridges is a world record breaking 41.58 kilometres and the project cost £5.4 billion.

An even bigger bridge and tunnel complex is planned to link Hong Kong, Zhuhai and Macau in 2016, with a total length of 50 kilometres.

BIG ENGINEERING

The Chang Jiang is the world's third longest river, with a length of 6,418 kilometres. It carries melting snow from the Qinghai-Tibet plateau eastwards to the sea, powering its way through the beautiful Three Gorges region to the east of Chongqing. Its lower reaches are broad and slow, spilling across the great plain. The Chang Jiang basin drains 20 per cent of all China and provides a home to one-third of the population. For nearly a century Chinese politicians and engineers dreamed of taming the power of this mighty river, controlling its floods and generating power.

THREE GORGES DAM

Between 1994 and 2012 that dream was made a reality, at the cost of about £25 billion. The river was dammed beneath the Three Gorges, with a two kilometre wall of concrete creating a reservoir 600 kilometres long. By controlling the amount of water in the reservoir, the danger of severe flooding downstream was much reduced, and conditions for shipping were improved. The Three Gorges Hydroelectric dam has 32 generators, each weighing about 6,000 tonnes, which can produce as much electricity as 11 nuclear power stations.

The Three Gorges Dam was the world's largest power station in terms of capacity in 2012.

Tamed at last, the waters of the Chang Jiang form a massive reservoir across the river valley.

CONCERNS

The dam project was a remarkable feat of engineering, but it has been widely criticised. Scenically, the rising water levels above the dam have reduced the impressive height of the Three Gorges. The huge mass of the reservoir is believed to have triggered landslides in the local area. The reservoir is also acting as a trap for industrial chemicals and city waste from upstream, forming a toxic lake.

THE HUMAN COST

The new reservoir drowned 13 cities, 140 towns and 1,350 villages. Many historical and archaeological sites were flooded. Over 1.2 million people were forced from their homes, and many farmers and fishermen lost their work. Officials suppressed protest and too often compensation was not paid.

A farmer watches on as the great dam is constructed. The displacement of people will swell the population of huge cities such as Chongqing.

25

AGAINST NATURE?

China's landscape has been shaped by human activity over the ages, but population growth and the spread of towns and factories are damaging the environment as never before. Such changes threaten the survival of many wild animals, such as the South China tiger, the Chinese alligator and the giant panda.

AIR POLLUTION

China's factories use a lot of coal, oil and gas. Over 50 per cent of Chinese power stations also rely on carbon-based fuels, making China the world's worst air polluter. Smog blankets cities, damaging health as well as the environment. The acid content of smoke mixes with rain, damaging plants and buildings. Many scientists fear that air pollution is causing global climate change and are trying to agree international cuts in carbon emissions. China feels that the developed countries which became rich through industrialising back in the 1800s should carry most of the cost, and give newcomers time to catch up. China does agree to programmes of carbon cutting, but many worry that these offer too little, too late.

Hunting and the loss of forests have endangered the South Chinese tiger. There now may be fewer than 20 tigers surviving in the wild, and none have actually been seen for over 25 years.

SOIL, WIND AND WATER

In many regions China's soil is in a bad way. Often the land is over-farmed and treated with too much chemical fertiliser. As cities spread out into the countryside, forests are cut down, and there are no longer roots to hold the soil and keep it moist. It turns to dust and blows away with the wind. Deserts are spreading. As more and more water is needed, there can be severe shortages.

Since 1948, 20 per cent of farmland has been lost to erosion or urban development. For a country which relies on home-grown crops to feed its growing population, that poses a serious danger.

A GREENER CHINA

China is taking steps to make things better. Some of the more polluting power plants have been shut down. A massive 22 per cent of China's power is already generated by hydro-electric schemes and 2.3 per cent from other renewable sources, such as sun and wind. China is now a world leader in the production, trading and installation of photovoltaic technology, which generates power from solar radiation. In recent years ordinary people across the country have become more aware of the environment, protesting in public against factory pollution, and taking part in tree-planting schemes.

China is investing in many tree-planting schemes. These are designed to halt the spread of the Gobi Desert into northern China.

SEEKING JUSTICE

China has had a low crime rate for many years. But there are signs that violent crime is on the increase. One reason for this may be the growing gap between rich and poor.

THE LAW

Many Chinese laws are similar to those in other countries, but the courts are not independent from government. The National People's Congress appoints judges to the Supreme Court and the interests of the state are seen as more important than individual rights. However, reforms were passed in 1996 and 2012, bringing in jurors and giving greater rights to defendants.

PUNISHMENT

Until 2014 China had many labour camps, where prisoners could spend up to four years without trial. These are now being closed down. Court sentences are often harsh.

Billionaire Chinese businessman Liu Han on trial for running a gang of loan sharks and contract killers. He was found guilty and executed in February 2015.

The number of crimes carrying the death penalty has been reduced, but is still very large. China is believed to execute thousands of convicted prisoners a year, more than any other country in the world. The exact number is kept secret.

HUMAN RIGHTS

International campaigners criticise China's record on human rights. They point to the lack of free speech and basic political or religious freedoms (see page 37). They criticise the system of justice and capital punishment, as well as the way in which dissidents may be shut away in psychiatric institutions. China's hardline treatment of campaigners for Tibetan independence has met with protests around the world.

Some leading Chinese figures have become famous for criticising government policies. The number of ordinary Chinese people who dare to protest about human rights is small, but their number is growing.

The popular artist and political activist Ai Weiwei has become a thorn in the flesh of the Chinese government.

AN ARTIST PROTESTS

Ai Weiwei (born 1957) is a Chinese artist and architect. He is best known as the artistic consultant for the National Stadium for the 2008 Beijing Olympics (see page 15).

However Ai has become even better known as a critic of the Chinese record on human rights.

• He criticised the Olympic Games organisers.

• He blamed poor building standards for deaths in the 2008 Sichuan earthquake.

• He protested against air pollution in China's cities, photographing himself in a gas mask.

• He has mocked the Chinese government with photographs and performance art.

Over the years the Chinese authorities have responded by closing down Ai Weiwei's studio, charging him with not paying taxes, putting him in prison and refusing him foreign travel permits.

HEALTH AND LEARNING

When the first American burger chain opened in China in 1990, a customer was asked what he thought of the food. He looked puzzled and said, 'Is it supposed to taste like that?' These days Western fast foods are so familiar in the cities that they are causing a worrying rise in obesity. Another habit has caused a health problem for many years. China is the world's biggest producer of tobacco, and despite campaigns, the Chinese remain great smokers.

HEALTHCARE

Smoking and air pollution are two reasons why cancer, heart disease and breathing problems are common diseases in China. However, most Chinese women can expect to live to over 77 years old and men to about 73 years of age. China spends 5.6 per cent of its GDP on healthcare. City hospitals are better equipped than those in the country, but most villages have medical clinics. China has moved away from the communist ideal of free healthcare for all. This has led to hardship for poorer people, as welfare allowances are cut. A health insurance system is now in place, and private medical care is available for those who can afford it. China now works together with western nations in medical research and training.

American fast food on sale in Xianyang.
Increased prosperity is rapidly changing people's diet in China's cities.

HERBS AND ACUPUNCTURE

In China you can often see bundles of herbs and other traditional medications on sale. Acupuncture, treatment with fine needles, is another popular way of dealing with medical problems.

LEARNING

Education has a very ancient history in China. The tradition is to learn by rote and then be tested. There is less emphasis on individualism or challenging questions. Children have to spend at least nine years at school. Primary education lasts from the age of 6 or 7 until 12, and secondary schools are attended between 12 and 18. There used to be no private schools in China, but these now exist and are used by wealthier families, in another departure from communist principles for the government. Recent years have seen a great increase in study at the country's 2,000 universities and colleges, which have about six million student places. Rising fees have hit poorer students, despite a loans scheme. Wealthier students may study at private colleges or overseas.

LITERACY LEAP

While children in Europe or the USA may struggle with an alphabet of 26 letters, Chinese school children must learn at least 3–4,000 characters! These are symbols which represent words or sounds. Before 1949, 80 per cent of the population could not read or write. Today over 95 per cent of people over the age of 15 are literate.

Jars of traditional Chinese medicines. Some of these treatments have been used in China for over 2,000 years.

MEDIA MESSAGES

The Chinese have been writing for over 3,000 years, and their literature includes poetry and many novels. Paper was invented in China 2,000 years ago, and what may be the oldest printed book in the world to have survived, the *Diamond Sutra*, was published in China in 868. About 600 years ago China produced the Wikipedia of its day, an encyclopedia known as the *Yongle Dadian*. It was produced by 2,000 scholars and written on scrolls making up 11,095 volumes!

Newspaper and magazine sales in China are still rising, while they are falling in Europe and North America.

MAINSTREAM MEDIA

Words are still spinning off China's printing presses today. Over 96 million national and regional newspapers are sold every day in China and magazine sales are rising. About 8.3 billion books are printed each year. Other communications media are booming too. Television and radio offer over 3,000 channels or stations at national, provincial or city level. All are owned or approved by the Communist Party or the state, and journalists who step out of line risk imprisonment (see opposite).

Customers log on at an Internet cafe in Chengdu, Sichuan province. The meteoric rise of the Internet is being monitored closely by the government.

POLICING THE PRESS

In January 2013, about 100 journalists working on the Guangdong newspaper *Southern Weekend* went on strike. In most countries such a scene would not be unusual, but in China this news was sensational.

- Why did the journalists stop work? The propaganda chief for Guangdong province had axed an article in the newspaper calling for human rights to be protected. He replaced it with an article praising the Chinese Communist Party. The journalists claimed he had misrepresented them on the newspaper's microblog, and said that over 1,000 articles in the paper had been censored in the previous year.

- What did the public think? A crowd of sympathisers soon gathered outside the newspaper offices. Students, lawyers and other journalists all expressed their support.

- Were the strikers punished? It was agreed that no action against them would be taken, so they returned to work. However Internet access to sites reporting this story was blocked.

CHINA ONLINE

It is much easier for governments to control and regulate traditional publishing and broadcasting than the new electronic media. China has an incredible 1.3 billion mobile phones. It has more Internet users than any other nation – about 626.6 million. Many writers self-publish online, and there is great enthusiasm for popular fiction. A huge number of Internet users log into a microblogging site called Sina Weibo. It is like Twitter and gets about 100 million messages posted every day. Sina Weibo is a symbol of just how much China has changed, and is itself speeding up that change.

THE GREAT FIREWALL OF CHINA

It is hard for any one nation to control or censor the media in the global age of the Internet. China has shut down websites and blocked access to foreign media sites as well as Facebook and Twitter. This policy has been called 'the Great Firewall of China'. Like the Great Wall itself, it is unlikely to be able to hold back outside influences for ever.

ARTS AND ARENAS

The way in which people express and enjoy themselves can reveal a great deal. China has a rich culture which has evolved over thousands of years. Its common themes include a love of harmony, balance and simple beauty, all ideas which are deeply rooted in ancient spiritual beliefs.

ART AND CRAFT

The first Chinese poetry was closely linked with music. Writing merged with the visual arts in calligraphy, the beautiful painting of Chinese characters or symbols. Chinese craft skills also produced the fine pottery called porcelain and luxurious silk textiles.

Chinese music was very different from European music, and could be graceful, or dramatic with crashing gongs, bells and drums. Performance arts included acrobatics, juggling and popular Chinese operas in which heroes and villains with painted faces or masks and elaborate costumes play out dramatic tales.

CULTURE AND CHANGE

In the 1950s and 60s Western styles of art and music were frowned upon, but Chinese arts such as calligraphy were encouraged. However, all the arts were expected to serve Communist ideals. Traditional Chinese operas were updated as revolutionary propaganda.

Today, artists in China have greater freedom. Chinese art has become very popular internationally, as has the work of film-makers. Films such as the action comedy *Let the Bullets Fly*, directed by Jiang Wen in 2010, have been hugely popular with the Chinese public. Other film makers are taking on social issues such as migration into the cities. Artists making political statements still need to be very careful, however.

Drama and colour... A traditional opera called 'Monkey King: Flaming Mountain' is staged by the Sichuan Opera Theatre company.

LEISURE

Parks are often the best place to see how people in China spend their leisure time. They may gather to make music, play cards or have a game of Chinese chess. You may see people practising the slow moves of taijiquan (*tai chi*), a traditional martial art which is also a good way to relax and keep fit.

SPORT

Table tennis is a popular sport in China, and China has produced many internationally successful players. The Beijing Olympics of 2008 put Chinese sport under the international spotlight and gave a big boost to badminton, basketball, volleyball and swimming. Beijing is now scheduled to host the 2022 Winter Olympics. At the highest level of football, city-based clubs compete in a Chinese Super League, while Chinese football fans also often follow the European game.

Synchronised diving champions Chen Ruolin and Wang Xin celebrate winning gold at the 2008 Beijing Olympics.

A great way to start the day. Taijiquan helps to relieve the stress of city life.

BELIEFS AND FESTIVALS

Emei Shan, in Sichuan province, is one of China's holy mountains. Walking up trails through its forests, you come across beautiful old Buddhist temples with incense sticks placed before statues. Emei Shan may seem to be a world away from the materialistic world of the big cities, but traditional beliefs have always shaped Chinese society, and still do.

The Golden Summit at the top of Mount Emei. Mount Emei is regarded as one of the four sacred Buddhist mountains in China.

THREE TRADITIONS

Three philosophies took root in China in ancient times – Daoism, Confucianism and Buddhism. They existed alongside each other until they gradually intertwined and became seen as paths to the same truth. They developed rituals and religious ceremonies, sometimes mixing with much older beliefs in spirits and magic. It was from the teachings of Lao Zi, Kong Fuzi (Confucius) and Gautama Buddha, the founder of Buddhism, that the Chinese developed an understanding of the natural way of the world, respect for ancestors, ideals of compassion and duties to family and nation. Buddhism took many forms in China, with a separate branch of the faith developing in Tibet, Mongolia and northeast China.

The Chinese New Year is the biggest festival of the year, and is celebrated around the world.

RELIGION AND POLITICS

In 1949 the new Communist government was officially atheist, claiming that religions such as Confucianism held back social progress. During the Cultural Revolution (the period of political unrest in the 1960s) activists tried to ban all worship and destroy religious buildings. Many of these have now been restored. President Xi Jinping himself is known to admire the Confucian tradition. Today religious worship is permitted and nearly one third of China's population may be religious believers. Five main Chinese-based religious organisations (Buddhist, Daoist, Protestant, Catholic and Muslim) are officially recognised, but unregistered sects may be harassed by the authorities, and so choose to worship in secret.

ISLAM AND CHRISTIANITY

Islam arrived in China in the 7th century BCE. Today, there is still a large Chinese Muslim community known as the Hui. Their Grand Mosque is in the historic city of Xian, in the northwest province of Shaanxi. Islam is also the religion followed by Uyghurs and Tajiks living in China's far west. Christianity arrived at around the same time as Islam, and was mostly spread by Western missionaries in the 1800s and 1900s.

FIRECRACKERS AND DRAGONS

Most Chinese people today are not religious, although they are often superstitious about lucky numbers or good fortune. They also enjoy seasonal and regional festivals. The Chinese New Year is celebrated with firecrackers, drums, cymbals and dragon and lion dances.

FOCUS ON BEIJING

RELAX!

Even in times of hardship the Chinese people have always managed to find ways of enjoying themselves through music, performance, art or simple fun. These days Beijing offers more entertainment possibilities than ever before.

A symbol of change can be seen in Dashanzi, in Beijing's Chaoyang district. Here a former military factory space has been taken over as a lively centre of international artistic creativity known as the 798 Art Zone.

Beijing's theatres offer traditional, spectacular Beijing operas, as well as circus skills or martial arts diplays. At the Beijing Dance Academy, students learn classical ballet.

China is famous for its tasty cuisine, and most of its regional styles of food can be tried in Beijing, whose own claim to fame is crispy roasted duck. Popular restaurants offer a huge choice of dishes, which seem to make use of every possible part of an animal or plant. Nothing goes to waste in a Chinese kitchen!

In winter families might go skating in Beihai Park, or in the spring take a boat out on the lake at Yiheyuan (the New Summer Palace). And an old man might sit on a bench in the summer sunshine, with his memories – and his caged birds.

Visitors get into the exhibits at the 798 Art Zone, a centre of experimental painting and sculpture.

When the lake freezes over in Beihai Park, it's time to wrap up warm and go skating. In January daytime temperatures may be just above freezing point, dropping to about −9°C overnight.

A group of friends meets up for an open air lunch on a sunny day in Beijing.

The er hu is a traditional two-stringed fiddle, played with a bow. It may be heard in parks and on the streets, where it is often played by blind buskers.

Keeping caged birds is a traditional hobby in China. You can often see older men taking their pets to the park for some sunshine and fresh air.

39

CHINA INTERNATIONAL

Chinese workers have settled in other parts of the world for hundreds of years. In many cities, from London to San Francisco, from Singapore to Sydney, there are long established Chinese communities, markets, businesses and cultural centres. Chinese languages are spoken as a first language by about 1,213,000,000 people worldwide. Now that China itself has opened up to the outside world, its international role is more important than ever.

Chinatown in San Francisco is home to the oldest Chinese community in the United States, dating back to 1848.

TRADE AND RESOURCES

New links are most often based upon business, trade and investment. If trade does not flow both ways equally there can be problems. The United States buys far more Chinese goods than China buys American goods, for example. Still, business relationships can have other advantages, leading towards cooperation in education, sciences, the arts or sports. China and Britain agreed a new programme of cooperation in 2015.

China's search for resources has been on a massive scale, so the recent slowdown of its economy has affected mining and other industries worldwide. China still owns farms and factories from Africa to South America. Such business deals are often welcomed, especially if they bring another country much needed roadbuilding and development, but at times they can lead to tensions with local communities and workers (see box on page 41).

Local workers sort ore under Chinese supervision, at a depot in the Katanga region of the Democratic Republic of Congo.

CHINESE IN AFRICA

Chinese ships have been visiting Africa since the Middle Ages. Today natural resources such as oil and metals have attracted many Chinese companies. When China's use of metals soared in the boom years, it invested heavily in Zambia's copper mines. Their investment was welcomed, but there were soon disputes over wages.

As the Chinese economy slowed down, demand for copper fell. In 2015 Chinese companies in Zambia faced two problems. Drought was reducing the hydroelectric power they needed for electricity for mining machinery, and copper prices were falling. Output from the mines was reduced and Zambian workers began to be laid off.

MAPS AND BORDERS

Most countries have disputes about their borders from time to time. China shares its frontiers with no fewer than 14 other nations. In the past there have been border disputes with India, Russia and Vietnam, but these are now settled.

Rivalry for offshore oil reserves is now causing new disputes, with Southeast Asian nations arguing about maritime boundaries and the ownership of islands in the South China Sea. Although Japan and China are big trading partners, there are historical tensions between the two, rooted in the Japanese invasions from 1931 to 1945.

'TAIWAN, PROVINCE OF CHINA'

Taiwan is another political flashpoint. The Nationalist Chinese set up a government on this island when the Communists came to power in Beijing in 1949. Taiwan claimed to represent the whole of China and was strongly supported by the United States. In turn the People's Republic claimed Taiwan as one of its provinces. From time to time military exercises along the Taiwan Strait still raise international tension.

41

LOOKING TO THE FUTURE

Coming down to Earth. Liu Yang waves as she emerges from the re-entry capsule, after her space flight.

On 16 June 2012 Liu Yang became the first Chinese woman in space. Her spacecraft, *Shenzhou 9*, was launched by rocket from the Gobi Desert. It docked with the *Tiangong 1* space station two days later. Liu Yang was born in 1978, just two years after the death of Mao Zedong. Her life has matched almost exactly the rise of China as a great economic power. Her achievement showed just how far China has advanced its technology.

BIG QUESTIONS

The Chinese philosopher Lao Zi wrote: 'The flame that burns twice as bright burns half as long.' China's future could be very bright, but nothing is certain. Can China find the resources it needs? Can it pay higher wages and still compete internationally? Can it develop further without ruining the environment and its heritage? If China makes political reforms, will it still be able to direct its economy as effectively? China is spending large amounts of money on the military. Can it live in peace with its neighbours? Can this country manage a society which is divided by wealth, or can it build a more equal and just society, respecting human rights?

WAYS FORWARD

All these questions apply not just to China, but to nations around the world. Sustainability, the environment, economics, growth and human rights are issues for us all. If there is a difference, it is the sheer size and the scale of the problems for the world's biggest population. As Liu Yang looked back at the Earth, she would have seen the planet looking small in the vastness of space. That image always reminds us that we must work together for a better future. What kind of nation China will become is unknown, but if we look at over 2,000 years of history, three themes stand out from China's past – resilience, inventiveness and continuity.

Fishing with tame cormorants on the River Li. As China moves forward, it must value and take strength from its ancient traditions.

GLOSSARY

acupuncture a method of treating pain or illness using fine needles

authoritarian placing obedience to the government above personal freedoms

autonomous region a part of China which has regional government, with rights to pass some of its own laws

basin an area of land drained by a river and its tributaries

calligraphy handwriting as a form of art

capital (1) the chief city in a nation or region, often the centre of government (2) wealth in the form of money or property, used for business or finance

capitalism an economic system based on private ownership and the accumulation of private wealth

census an official count of the population

character a symbol which represents a sound or word in the Chinese language

climate change a change in the climate experienced in a region or in the world as a whole

colony a country or territory governed or settled by another nation

communications media any method of communicating, such as broadcasting, books, newspapers, cinema, television or the Internet

communism a social and economic system based on common ownership or state control in the interest of working people

corruption dishonest behaviour, such as accepting bribes

Cultural Revolution an attempt to rally radical support for Mao Zedong in the period 1966–68. This resulted in social chaos, violence and destruction

defendant the accused person during a trial

delta an area where silt has built up at a river mouth, creating a number of separate waterways

democracy a political system which represents the people

dissident somebody who disagrees with the government or society

emission the release of gases into the atmosphere, such as exhaust fumes from traffic

empire lands that have been brought together under the rule of a single government or emperor

erosion the wearing down of a landscape by wind, water, frost or heat

ethnic group part of a population sharing the same way of life, customs, beliefs, ancestry or language

faction a small group within a political party or government

firewall in computing, hardware or software which keeps a network secure or isolated

GDP (Gross Domestic Product) the total value of goods and services produced within a country in a year

human rights the basic needs required for people to be treated with justice and equality

hydroelectric power generated from the movement of water

innovation bringing in new ideas or technologies

investment putting money into an enterprise in order to make more money

labour camp a camp where prisoners are forced to carry out hard work, such as breaking stones

literate able to read and write

lock a section of a river or canal with a barrier, allowing boats to be lowered or raised from one level to another

Maglev A magnetic levitation system used for operating trains. Magnets raise the train from the rails, reducing friction

migrant labourer somebody who moves from one part of the country to another in search of work

missionary a religious person sent abroad to spread the faith

municipality in China, a division of regional government based upon a large city and the surrounding countryside

nationalise to place a private company or service under state ownership

nationalist 1) someone campaigning for their land to become independent or free of foreign control 2) someone promoting the interest of their own nation above all others

nationality in China, an ethnic or religious group recognised as having a particular legal status

natural resource any naturally occurring material which can be used in manufacturing or supply, such as coal, iron, water or timber

navigable of rivers, lakes or seas, able to be navigated by a ship

obesity being overweight

paddy field an area of flooded land used for growing rice

philosophy the study of knowledge, existence, truth and wisdom

photovoltaic converting rays from the Sun into electricity

plateau an expanse of flat land set at a high altitude

poverty line the lowest level of income required to meet basic needs

propaganda information or misinformation designed to promote a political party or a government, or used to denigrate opponents

prosecution the lawyers or other legal officials who make the case against defendants in courts of law

province in China, a region of administration and local government

reach an open stretch of a winding river course

renewable not depending on resources which will run out. Wind, sun and waves are all renewable energy sources

republic a country ruled by the people rather than by a king, queen or emperor

reservoir an area or containment used to store a large mass of water

rote learning words, facts or figures off by heart

shareholder someone who buys shares in a company, in order to make money from the company's profits

social media online sites which encourage the exchange of information and ideas between individuals and groups

Special Administrative Regions parts of China which have their own economic and political system, namely the former colonies of Macau (Portugal) and Hong Kong (Britain)

Special Economic Zone a region of China which encourages foreign investment and the development of new industries

steppes wide open areas of natural grassland

stock exchange a financial centre for the buying and selling of shares

sub-tropical bordering the Earth's tropical regions

Supreme Court in many countries, the name given to the highest court of law

toxic poisonous

trade gap the difference between the value of imports and exports

tuberculosis an infectious disease which often damages the lungs

typhoon a tropical storm, the East Asian name for a hurricane

visual arts arts based on appearance, such as painting, photography or sculpture

welfare economic or other support given to an individual or family by the state

FURTHER INFORMATION

BOOKS

Journey Through: China (Franklin Watts, 2016)

Countries in our World: China, Oliver James (Franklin Watts, 2013)

Modern China: A Very Short Introduction, Rana Mitter (OUP, 2016)

WEBSITES

http://news.bbc.co.uk/1/shared/ spl/hi/in_depth/china_modern/ html/1.stm
A simple introduction to China.

http://www.guardian.co.uk/ world/interactive/2012/mar/23/ china-decade-change-interactive- timeline
A very useful interactive timeline showing events from recent Chinese politics, economics, development and other areas of interest.

http://www.chinatoday.com
A busy portal with links to Chinese and international media and to a very wide range of topics.

http://travel.nationalgeographic. co.uk/travel/countries/china-guide
Pictures and articles on ancient and modern China, Chinese culture and travel.

INDEX